# UNDERSTANDING
## Illegal Immigration

## The Wall and All It Stands For

**Frank N. Mitchell**

This UNDERSTANDING booklet is part of a series of booklets on key issues of our time on the Reign of Christ at
www.ashiningcityonahill.org
www.reignofchrist.org
All booklets are available at amazon.com

August 2018

# Preface

This UNDERSTANDING booklet is one in a series of booklets concerning **THE REIGN OF CHRIST** for our time and how that Reign plays out in all history and as foretold in the Bible.

The problem that I have encountered over the last 30 or 40 years is that Christians who think we should be praying and working for the Kingdom to come on Earth (in order to have the thousand year Reign of Christ in all its fullness) are generally Liberals and apostates who have a false and counterfeit Social Gospel and Social Justice message and understanding of the Kingdom come on Earth and of any possible millennial era of Christ.

On the other hand solid Bible-believing Christians, for a variety of reasons, often tend to be what are called amillennialists and premillennialists, and these folks generally think we are *not* to be praying or working for the Kingdom outside of some minor evangelism and works of charity. Their view is, tragically, that Jesus told us to hunker down in the churches and to wait for Him to return and for this current age to end or the world to end as we know it.

The practical importance of all of this cannot be overstated. It means few if any conservative Bible commentators are really thinking about what it would mean for the Kingdom of God to come on

Earth in all its fullness in the much prophesied worldwide Reign of Christ.

And to further complicate these matters there are many aspects to an actual Kingdom Era come here on planet Earth, and there are many obstacles to how such a Kingdom might well play out in actual history. And, finally, for a true Kingdom come on Earth there are many interrelated political, religious and economic difficulties and confusions in our time to be resolved and overcome.

Given this situation, each booklet in this UNDERSTANDING series tends to stand on its own in order to address some given specific problem or set of problems concerning a coming millennial era on Earth where we will see the nations or "kingdoms of this world become the kingdoms of our Lord and of His Christ."

In this coming time, *each shall know the Lord from the least to the greatest* and *the knowledge of God will fill the whole world as waters cover the sea*. And in this Kingdom time, we will see, worldwide, true worship of God in Spirit and Truth, and we will see all the nations in harmonious interaction in Peace, Justice, and Righteousness.

This will then be the much prophesied and long anticipated reign of the Son of David in a worldwide Reign of Christ.

Frank Mitchell

4

# UNDERSTANDING
## Illegal Immigration
### The Wall and All It Stands For

Perhaps no two words sum up the phenomenon of Donald Trump more than "the wall." Probably, no issue concerning Donald Trump has been more reported on and misreported on than "the wall." In its own way "the wall" tends to encapsulate in two words, for both his supporters and his opponents, everything that is both good or bad about the man and what he stands for. I would like in this little booklet to look at why that is the case as I, in August of 2018, reflect back over his campaign and now his presidency to date.

**Illegal immigrants and crime**
The wall was the first big issue from the very beginning of Donald Trump's campaign, and it dealt with the twofold problem of people being in this country illegally and the fact that there is also much crime and drug dealing associated with the millions of illegal aliens in the country, who are sometimes just called "illegals" for short. The Democrats like to use the false euphemism "undocumented workers" for illegals, but that label is very inaccurate because many of the illegals are not working, and it is not as if they just happened not to have filled out the right paper work or documents when they snuck into the

country. So, for the sake of clarity and accuracy, we here will refer to the illegal aliens or illegal immigrants by traditional terminology.

In the summer of 2015 the thing that struck this writer about Donald Trump was that when he started talking about the wall, it did not seem to me to be much of an issue or controversial issue. Why? All people and all politicians, both Republicans and Democrats, have said for years that they wanted a wall, a fence or secure border. To my knowledge not a single political candidate (until the last few months) has said he or she was for the generally open border or unsecure border that we have today and have had for years.

Every politician, it seems from the beginning of time, promises to fix all the society's problems, and in America for the past 30 years a wall or a fence to secure what is generally seen to be an open border is just part of the litany of issues to be dealt with by any candidate if elected. So what was the big deal about Trump that caused all of the stir? Trump exposed the fact that apparently virtually all of the major politicians of **both** political parties over the last 30 years since Reagan ran in 1984 have been lying to the American people. They have not had the slightest intention of securing the border, wall or no wall, and of course the mainstream media has known this fact for the past 30 years and never reported it, thus making them once again what Trump calls "fake news" on this issue as on so many others.

Trump not only exposed all the lying major politicians on this big issue of national security and national well-being, but he also introduced honesty back into American politics and a presidential campaign in a way we have not seen in America since 1984! This was no small accomplishment!

People went crazy over Trump both for and against him, not for what he said, but for the fact he seemed to really mean what he said about a secure border and a wall. He was, in effect, on this major issue going to do what every other candidate had been promising to do one way or another for over thirty years, but they had not had the slightest intention of doing anything about securing the border and restoring the rule of law to our nation. So, one must ask, "A wall, what's the big deal?"

**Globalism and Open Borders**
A central part of the globalist agenda *against* free and sovereign states is "open borders" with an inevitable accompanying open immigration, even migration and lawlessness, and tragically so, as even G. H. W. Bush openly sought in 1990 in his famous New World Order UN speech. This means unless one wishes to, in effect, dissolve the nation-state and any and all meaningful national identity and citizenship one *cannot* have the globalist policy of open borders, but the people of America have *never* voted to implement these open-border globalist policies.

However, open borders, open immigration, no nation-states and no national identity are part of the United Nations vision for the world that the US foolishly bought into when the UN was formed after World War II. In fact, Barack Obama openly ran for president as a "citizen of the world," and no Democrats or globalist Republicans had a problem with it, and neither did the mainstream fake news, who, as I recall, never even mentioned Obama and Americans as "citizens of the world," let alone questioned it.

In fact, if you look at the never-Trump Republicans, everyone of them that I have investigated is a well-known globalist who believes in no wall, open borders, amnesty, and a "pathway to citizenship" for virtually all illegal aliens. A "pathway to citizenship" is a euphemism for amnesty with a $1000 fine. And, of course, in the world and alternative universe of the pc globalist, anyone who is not for lawlessness, open borders, open immigration, open citizenship, and no wall is a so-called "far right nationalist" and a "xenophobe," supposedly not reflecting "the values" of America. How many times has this been said by Democrats, the media, and globalist Republicans about Trump and his millions of supporters? Too many to count.

In fact, this pretty much is how you know if someone is a globalist and never-Trumper; he or she is a no-wall person and against all the wall stands for. This is a curious thing. Everyone, like Trump, **who**

**believes in traditional American values and the rule of law** is supposedly far right, un-American and even un-Constitutional of all things, but why is this? The answer is because the radical multiculturalism and non-assimilation of the Left (which open borders and lawlessness bring with them) are the new norms and "American values" for all Democrats and for all anti-Trump globalist Republicans.

**Non-assimilation as the new "American value"**
Traditionally the whole point of coming to America was to assimilate into our great American culture and values and to learn English, and to this ends one swore allegiance to the American Constitution as written, but these goals of immigration are no longer the case for all globalists and all Democrats. For all globalists and all Democrats the point of coming to America has become **non-assimilation** and *not* learning English and *not* embracing the Constitution as written. For decades, at least since Ronald Reagan, the Democrats have openly opposed any Supreme Court nominee who believed in the Constitution as written and supported any nominee with a record of *not* believing in the Constitution as written but rather its Social Justice opposite as infamously proposed by FDR in 1944.

For the Democrat of at least the last 30 years, the Constitution "lives" to mean virtually anything, even its opposite! This is very Orwellian. This is Alice-in-Wonderland constitutional law. It is arguably THE major story in America for the last three decades!

How many stories has the mainstream fake news run on this huge problem our nation has faced for over a generation? To my knowledge not a single one. Why? Stories on this crisis do not support the globalist, lawless, un-American agenda of the Democrats, which by definition is un-Constitutional. Instead, the mainstream fake news has created a whole new lexicon to describe traditional Americans and traditional American values.

We all know the routine. We hear it day after day from Democrats, globalist Republicans, and the mainstream fake news. Trump and all of his traditional American followers are not simply xenophobes and far right nationalists but deplorable and prejudiced. They are racist and sexist and bigots and Islamophobes and homophobes and every other phobe one can think of and of course unloving. Why? Because the Democrats and globalist Republicans believe in agape love as lawlessness.

This is a classic Gnostic heresy of Liberals in many, many churches. How many times have we heard from Democrats, globalist Republicans, and religious leaders that we should have open borders, open immigration and amnesty along with radical multiculturalism and a bi-lingual nation because of a supposed Christian agape love as lawlessness? Innumerable times, of course. But it is worse than this, both for legal and illegal immigration.

**Islamic Sharia law, anyone?**
Not only for Democrats does the Constitution live to mean its Social Justice opposite to classical Justice, it also in our Orwellian, Alice-in-Wonderland world "lives" to mean Islamic Sharia "Justice." This is supposedly no problem even for legal immigrants! However, a main purpose of the US Constitution as stated in the Preamble is to "establish Justice." It is not, as FDR wanted, to establish its opposite Social Justice, and it is certainly not to establish the clear evil of Sharia "Justice."

Traditionally, one had to leave Sharia back in the home country if one came to America, and one had to embrace both the Justice of the Constitution **and** assimilation. However, today, and for the past 30 years the Justice of the Constitution and assimilation are the new un-American xenophobic evils and values of the far right, anti-globalist nationalist and of course of anyone who wants Trump to build his wall.

If you figure roughly 365 days times 30 years, the mainstream fake news has had well over 10,000 opportunities to have a story on this complete meltdown of traditional American values, the Constitution, and honesty in American politics, but they have apparently been too busy with their endless parroting of false narratives about conservatives and doing mere name calling day after day, week after week, and year after year. How does this work?

**Fake news, anyone?**
The mainstream media does not see itself as doing fake news of course. Why? Let's say someone calls Donald Trump a xenophobe or far right nationalist when he starts his campaign and when he starts talking about a wall or about the clear problems of illegal immigration. That is an unfair news story. It is not accurate, as we have seen, but it is a free country, and one can call people such things, even unfairly, in a political campaign if we have a free press.

However, such a story of xenophobe or far right nationalist should have had no legs, as the expression goes, but instead, for a host of politically correct reasons, such labels as "xenophobe" or "far right nationalist" became a factually false narrative that was then repeated on Trump or similar candidates over and over again. *If* one repeats a false narrative, one thinks, incorrectly, it is justified because one really and truly thinks that the false narrative is true and not fake. And to complicate matters anything today that is not politically correct globalist or radically multicultural is seen to be xenophobic and far right nationalist, un-American and so forth. And to make matters even worse, if one learns this Orwellian nonsense in college, one then is even more certain that the false labels are true and not false or "fake."

**Donald Trump's tweets**
Look at it this way: When the mainstream media, for whatever its reasons, does a lousy story, Donald

Trump, bless his heart, often sees it as what is known as "a teachable moment" for the American people and even for the mainstream media itself, and he, therefore, does a tweet on the story as "fake news." But when Trump does this the mainstream media is, of course, offended because it usually never crosses their minds that they are merely repeating or parroting some false narrative where they might take something completely out of context that Trump says and twist it to mean no telling what in their open animus for the man, which they think is justified because he is not politically correct.

However, for Trump's loyal followers that is the whole point; he is not simply repeating false politically correct narratives of the Democrats and globalist politicians concerning the wall and all it stands for or concerning anything else.

**Understanding "Human Rights"**
The fact is, the Democrats notwithstanding, there is no "human right" to immigrate into a country or to open borders or to citizenship or for asylum to anyone seeking it. The fact is such human rights notions are utterly, totally and completely ridiculous. And Trump merely points this out, in effect, and the mainstream media goes crazy with their name-calling. Think about it. The position of the Democrats is that virtually anyone who is standing on US soil, legally or illegally, has a human right to American citizenship. This is not only lawless but absurd. Think about it in reverse.

No one would claim that an American has a right to citizenship in France or Mexico just because that American is standing in France or Mexico, how ridiculous. And the same is true with so-called "anchor babies." Just having a child while being on American soil, legally or illegally, does not automatically entitle that child to citizenship, and it is ridiculous and absurd to read that into the Constitution, but the Democrats routinely read virtually **anything** into the Constitution for partisan political purposes, what's new?

So, what the solution? In the early 1930s and the early 1950s we had a similar problem with illegal immigrants, and literally millions were either deported or self-deported, and presumably that is what must happen again, not just to maintain the principle and rule of law, but to restore the national unity and identity against the radical multi-culturalism that is literally overwhelming us. If learning English is part of becoming a legal US citizen then presumably we are degenerating into a highly undesirable bi-lingual society simply because of the massive numbers of unassimilated illegal immigrants. In order to streamline things we may need special deportation courts or something similar as well as a wall, and many have suggested a virtual freeze on even legal immigration for a generation or two, that is, until we can assimilate the millions of legal immigrants already here into traditional American values and culture.

**The restoration of our American republic**

Of course, none of the restoration of our American republic or the restoration of our broken legal and illegal immigration system, with its de facto open-border policies and no secure-border policies, will happen with a wall or otherwise until we drain the swamp in Washington by sending the Democrats and globalist Republicans packing. The Democrats to a person are almost all obstructionists on these matters and generally even un-American (as traditionally defined) and even un-Constitutional (as traditionally defined), and the Democratic Party, though it has a noble past, has in recent decades become unrecognizable to that noble past, and it has, millions of Americans feel, outlived its constructive usefulness for our nation. For some reason very little, if any, of these monumental historical facts make it into the mainstream media. I'm not sure why, but this is why traditional Americans often see the mainstream media as generally fake news.

Bottom line? The Democratic Party should disband for the good of the nation, but they are probably not going to do that. So, they will have to be disbanded by the American voters getting on the Republican Trump train in the coming months and years in order to clean out the House and Senate from the Democratic obstructionist presence. This is a very sad and tragic situation, but for the good of the nation, it must be done. And in many ways "the wall," indeed, says it all in that it touches on almost all of the major issues of our time and on the issues that Trump is trying to address whether open borders, lawlessness, America-last globalism, crime, national security, radical multiculturalism, non-assimilation, false Constitutional law, false American moral values, and endless false news stories as well as the survival and restoration of our republic as we have known and loved it.

The subject of the wall and highly undesirable open mass immigration and migration also best represents the pattern of anti-Trump hysteria, animus, and misrepresentation that we see on almost every major issue today concerning Trump. This is sometimes called Trump Derangement Syndrome. Trump is never attacked or engaged on the issues by Democrats or the media where we see only endless name-calling and manufactured crises from Russian collusion to border family separations, from misreported G-7 talks to misreported Paris climate accords to the bad Iran nuclear deal that was a treaty called a non-treaty, etc. What is the pattern?

Trump's positions are not accurately reported day after day nor are his positions on what are actually non-globalist traditional American values, represented by the phrase "America first," which is what all nations do historically, that is, put their legitimate self-interest first, and this is true from the wall and immigration to false refugee crises to fair trade.

It is only in the last few decades that the nonsense of America-last globalism has taken hold with all Democrats and some establishment Republicans. In fact, fair trade proposed by Trump, where America is not taken advantage of, is called reactionary "protectionism," but as with a secure border, Trump's fair trade policies are virtually identical to those of candidate Bill Clinton in 1992 and candidate Barack Obama in 2008, where Clinton and Obama were hailed as American heroes, not villains, for their fair trade policies and agenda!

However, upon taking office both Clinton and Obama reversed themselves and embraced an un-American corporatist globalism, and not a word was heard in the press. Again, as with the wall and with mass open immigration, Trump has **not** reversed himself on fair trade in America's legitimate and even common sense self-interest, and his popularity soars with his supporters, who, one must hope and pray, will grow by the millions in the coming months and years for the sake of our truly great American values and our truly great nation that has served as A Shining City on a Hill for the whole world for over 200 years.

**Bottom-line: the two issues of our time**
The two major issues of our time are **one-world government** or **globalism**, which promotes open borders, and a false **one-world religion**, which also supports open borders and no walls, and both of these things (globalism government and one-world

religion) are supported by all Liberals and all Democrats. By contrast, Trump's main supporters are Evangelical Christians, and they support traditional concepts of national sovereignty, and they oppose both one-world government or globalism and one-world religion. The fact is though Trump's Evangelical supporters, as Trump, are called every rotten name in the book by the fake news, they generally know exactly what they believe and why on both issues of one-world government and one-world religion, and this is why they so strongly support Trump.

By contrast, for a variety of reasons, primarily blind loyalty to Democrats and Liberal causes, the mainstream media does not understand any of this nor any of the larger issues surrounding borders, a wall, true American values, diversity, non-assimilation, and so forth.

Regardless, and without any question, "the wall" stands for traditional American sovereignty and the rule of law and against the highly destructive policies and agenda of both political globalism and a one-world religion, which in fact *also* has a political agenda of open borders as well as an economic agenda of worldwide Socialist Justice incorporated into its religious agenda of merging all religions, all of which Trump's Evangelical supporters strongly oppose. "The wall," in a very real sense, is about making a stand against all of these issues of lawlessness, radical multiculturalism, and so forth.

**No small matter**
Sometimes issues in the news seem like just another daily crisis of some sort, but with the well-established globalism of the United Nations and the well-established World Council of Churches of the last seventy years, we have true crises of Biblical proportions.

We have an overtly clear political Babylon and religious Whore of Babylon of Revelation. What is more we have with Liberalism, humanism, atheism, and so forth an open rejection of the Higher Moral Law or, that is, the moral Laws of Nature, and we a rejection of the Creator God of that moral Law for what? For lawlessness.

Lawlessness is the spirit of anti-Christ in the Bible, and anyone who promotes lawlessness is a "man (or woman) of lawlessness." This is not pretty, but we must deal with reality as it is. Open borders and its globalism are by definition lawless. This is not even a close call.

Open borders and globalism are of an anti-Christ spirit, and they are invariably part of any Antichrist's agenda today. Why? The **political** issue of our time is globalism *versus* free sovereign states with Liberty and Justice for all. Trump and his supporters understand this, but his detractors do not, and they foolishly do not support Trump or his wall.

Further, the **religious** issue of our time is true worship of God in Spirit and Truth in Christian salvation, and this is *not* the apostate Liberal's agape love as lawlessness as we see in the end-time Laodicean church.

In short, the wall and all it stands for includes everything from the rule of law to traditional concepts of Justice and Righteousness to traditional understandings of love and Christianity to free and sovereign states fighting against the globalist anti-Christ agenda of lawlessness.

Promoting and voting for these grand and noble values against lawlessness are just as the American founders envisioned in their quest for our great nation to be a light to all nations and A Shining City on a Hill based on the moral Laws of Nature and of Nature's God, Wisely applied by the true statesman for the common good or general welfare of the commonwealth or, that is to say, the nation as a whole body politic.

===

Other booklets on the Reign of Christ in this UNDERSTANDING Series:

## UNDERSTANDING Prophecy Fulfillment:
### The Great Apostasy, Babylon, Mystery Babylon & the Reign of Christ

This little booklet gives an overview of the central major prophecies concerning the possible soon coming Reign of Christ. Specifically these are the prophecies of the Great Apostasy, Babylon, Mystery Babylon, and the man of lawlessness. These prophecies are seen as fulfilled in the false millennial visions of Marx and of the New World Order of UN Agenda 21 and Agenda 2030 and in the Liberal World Council of Churches.

## UNDERSTANDING All Bible Prophecy:
### Genesis to Revelation

This booklet holds that all prophecy should be interpreted in terms of the larger story of the Bible and the larger story of the Christian cosmology from the Creation to the Final Judgment, and this is especially the case for the book of Revelation.

## UNDERSTANDING Globalism:
### What is the "New World Order"?

This booklet looks at what "globalism" is generally and at the related topic of a "New World Order" that actually has *very* specific definitions and formulations that are often not well-known.

## UNDERSTANDING Revelation 19:
### Victory over One-World Government and One-World Religion

Revelation 19 though very controversial is actually very straightforward. The saints in a Marriage Supper of the Lamb move into a new more mature, intimate, and complete relationship with Christ, and then the saints in Christ and Christ in the saints completely and totally defeat the evils of one-world government and one-world religion. Simple enough when you get right down to it.

## UNDERSTANDING Statesmanship
### Classical Justice *versus* Social Justice

Probably no two notions are more misunderstood as well as more necessary to understand in our time than classical Justice and Social Justice. This booklet looks at the history of these two terms and how one stands for the Justice of statesmanship for doing the common good and the other for the injustice of special interest groups and wealth redistribution as a false human right for economic equality.

## UNDERSTANDING Alternative Political Universes:
### The Natural Revelation & Self-Evident Truths

For some folks as Jefferson and the American founders, the Natural Law or so-called Higher Moral Law is a self-evident truth, but for others with a reprobate mind and no common sense, this is not the case at all. These modern-day people who have lost their common sense are just as the ancient Epicureans (atheist hedonists) while modern-day Liberals are just as ancient Gnostics with their false enlightenment and false morality. Understand these things, and you will pretty well understand Alternative Political Universes.

## UNDERSTANDING Illegal Immigration:
### The Wall and All It Stands For

"The Wall" of Donald Trump stands for many larger issues from exposing hypocrisy among professional politicians to ending globalism, open borders, and the often total lawlessness of our time. Lawlessness of the Liberal and atheist-humanist is, in fact, the spirit of anti-Christ.

## UNDERSTANDING The Whole Counsel of the Kingdom:
### The Central Message of Jesus and Paul

Both Jesus and Paul preached a Whole Counsel of the Kingdom message, but this is not a generally well-known truth. This booklet looks at the concept of a Whole Counsel of the Kingdom Christianity and what it entails, namely, true worship of God in Spirit and Truth as well as Just and Righteous government.

## UNDERSTANDING Spiritual Warfare:
### Satan as a Roaring Lion

Scripture tells us that Satan goes about like a roaring lion seeking whom he may devour, but this is generally not a very understood warning, and tragically many people, if not devoured completely, get an arm or leg eaten (so to speak). To be forewarned is to be forearmed. This booklet deals with ways to recognize and deal with demons.

===

All of the above booklets are part of a series on key issues of our time on the Reign of Christ at
www.ashiningcityonahill.org
www.reignofchrist.org

All of the above booklets are put together is a single **Volume I** called

## UNDERSTANDING The Reign of CHRIST
### The One Big Issue of Our Time
### Volume I

This Volume I of all the above booklets together as well as all of the above booklets separately are available at **amazon.com**